Po

Treasures

To Earnestine,
5-11
God Bless, 2014
Icie A Jackson

Sandy Anderson

Mother of Pastor David
Icie Anderson Jackson *Anderson*

Mother's Day

Notice:

This book is a work of fiction, except for specific events or persons, which are mentioned. Otherwise, the poems depicting people, places, events and incidents are either a product of the authors' imagination or used fictitiously. Any resemblance to actual persons, living or dead, events, or locales is entirely coincidental.

Poetic Treasures. ©2013 by Sandy Anderson and Icie Anderson Jackson

Library of Congress Cataloging-in-Publications Data

ISBN: 9781490576022

Scripture quotations are from the Holy Bible, New King James Version (NKJV).

Design by Alexa Ayala

To order copies online, please go to www.amazon.com

Printed in the United States of America

First Edition

DEDICATION

As you read the poetry in this book, some may apply to a memory that you have or a situation in your own life. Our hope is that wherever you find yourself in life, you will take a few moments and allow yourself to be blessed by its' content. To all of those who have lived and are living out the words in our poems, this book is for you.

Table of Contents

Acknowledgements

There are a lot of people in a lot of places that make us who we are.
Sometimes these people are right up close and sometimes very far.
But thank you to all my family and friends for what you mean to me.
Without you in my life, how would I survive on this side of eternity?
My mother, Icie Anderson Jackson,
is a source of strength who always believed in me.

My fathers, Robert Anderson and Richard Jackson,
Who have been there guiding me.
Thanks to my sister, Brenda Anderson Fuller, who is a best friend to me.
To my brothers, Robert Anderson and David Anderson,
Who have always loved me.

But there were other friends and family, too,
Like Patricia Hill, Patrice Knowles, Ruby Johnson, Renee Butts and
Ann Maree W. Brown,
Who lifted me up, helped me out and constantly encouraged me.
There is a well in me that you all have helped set free.

And all my love to
Cassandra Joy McGraw Wittock and
Anthony "Jeffrey" McGraw, Jr.
You are the fruit of my womb and happiness for me.
But the greatest thanks goes to my deepest love,
The Christ of Calvary.

Sandy Anderson

Chapter 1

EXPRESSING FAITH AND HOPE

My Right To Be Who I Am

I can only be who I am.
You must accept me for being me.
I make no apologies for how God made me,
Or the person I choose to be.
It is my right as it is yours to be free.

Freedom is a state of mind.
I have the right to be this kind.
I have a whole life to live.
And I have a whole lot I can give.

We each are special and unique in our own way.
Everything in life has its day.
We must discover who we are,
And then we will know, just when it is our day.

To survive in this fast world.
We must be intimate with the calmness of our soul.
It is essential as a survival technique;
Or a necessity for every individual to seek.

In this world, I can only exist as all that I am.
I am made of parts from many.
Yet, I don't need to act like any
Because in me alone, there is plenty.

Sandy Anderson

POETIC TREASURES

"If you can envision it in your mind,

You can be all that you think you are."

For as he thinks in his heart, so is he.

Proverbs 23:7a NKJV

EXPRESSING FAITH AND HOPE

Be Your Dream

You can be your dream,
However impossible it may seem.
If you can imagine it in your mind,
Your dream can come true in time.

All you must do is believe.
Then, you can succeed.
In the goals that you perceive,
It is only a little faith you need.

If you have said, "I can't,"
You will never succeed.
But tell yourself, "I can."
Then, go for the mark, and be in the lead.

You can be your dream
Even if it seems afar.
If you can envision it in your mind,
You can be all that you think you are.

Sandy Anderson

POETIC TREASURES

"Prayer can change me,

And prayer can change you."

But Jesus looked at them and said to them,

"With men this is impossible,

but with God all things are possible."

Matthew 19:26

EXPRESSING FAITH AND HOPE

Labor Together

When its time to labor, and it pleases us not.
It maybe we are not cold, nor hot.
For laboring together should be our goal,
Striving along the way to save souls.

When others won't do right,
They refuse to change but rather fight.
Prayer changes people's attitudes, hearts and minds, too.
Prayer can change me,
And prayer can change you.

So pray on, be sincere, and be persistent.
God will get you through.
Because as we labor together from year to year,
There is enough work for all to share.
Laboring together should be our aim.
Working and praying in Jesus name.

Icie Anderson Jackson

"It is only by the freedom of my acts,

That you can truly know me."

EXPRESSING FAITH AND HOPE

See Me

When you look at me and wonder,
Why I do what it is I do.
I can only respond by saying,
Even as I am different,
What you observe is a part of you.

I respond to what I see, smell, taste, and feel.
But only the core of me is real.
Just as a dove flies freely,
It is only by the freedom of my acts,
That you can truly know me.

Be who you are separate from me.
As I shall live as a separate entity from thee.

Sandy Anderson

"Even when your heart aches with pain

Reach

When your mind trembles on the edge of sane

Reach"

Ask, and it will be given to you; seek, and you will

find; knock, and it will be opened to you.

Matthew 7:7   NKJV

EXPRESSING FAITH AND HOPE

Reach

When the worries of life have absorbed your thoughts
Reach
At times when only evil seems to be sought
Reach
Even when your heart aches with pain
Reach
When your mind trembles on the edge of sane
Reach
At the moment when you have spent your last dime
Reach
And you find out your husband has to serve time
Reach
Even when you are all dismay
Reach
And you look in the mirror at a head full of gray
Reach
And your innocent young daughter has learned to smoke
Reach
And your middle child has somewhere in life got choked
Reach
Even when your lights are turned off
Reach
And your bank reprocesses your house and car
Reach
And you question your worth and who you are
Reach
Remember, every nightmare has an end
So reach for the Son, as the dawn begins.

Sandy Anderson

"But how wonderful it would be if we could only

See why we should leave our baggage in

Yesterday, and begin dawn as a brand new day!"

...But one thing I do, forgetting those things which

are behind and reaching forward to those things

which are ahead. I press toward the goal...

Philippians 3:13

EXPRESSING FAITH AND HOPE

At the Dawn of Day

At the dawn of day life is new.
All that dawns with it is from yesterday.
All of our cares,
All of our fears,
All of our worries,
We brought from yesterday.
If only the things of yesterday could stay behind,
And we could start each day afresh.
Yet, we bring all of our baggage of yesterday into
The break of dawn.
But how wonderful it would be if we could only see,
Why we should leave our baggage in yesterday,
And begin dawn as a brand new day!

Sandy Anderson

"For my heart belongs to God;

The Creator of my being.

For my heart belongs to Him.

I owe Him everything."

EXPRESSING FAITH AND HOPE

For My Heart Belongs To God

I have traveled near and far
Looking for someone who could handle my emotions,
Only to find that Jesus alone,
Gives unconditional devotion.

In and out of relationships,
Investigating different creeds,
Not wanting to acknowledge that for Jesus,
The Spirit had already planted a seed.

A waste of time only to discover
That in this life, there is no other
Who could love me so deeply,
And answer all my longings so completely.

Thank you, Lord, for now I know
That there is one to meet my need.
One to forever hold me,
And to insure that I succeed.

What can I give for such a precious gift?
With all my soul and spirit,
To you, Lord, I uplift.

For my heart belongs to God;
The Creator of my being.
For my heart belongs to Him.
I owe Him everything.

Sandy Anderson

'Trust Christ as your Lord this very day.

Time is drawing nigh, and the hour is at hand.

For Jesus to return from His Heavenly land."

...We shall not all sleep, but we shall all be

changed in a moment, in the twinkling of an eye,

at the last trumpet.

I Corinthians 15:51-52 NKJV

EXPRESSING FAITH AND HOPE

What A Difference Christ Made In My Life

What a difference Jesus has been to me.
You see, from the bondage of my limitations,
I have been set free.
Through His grace and power,
I now have liberty.

Because of His presence,
I have joy that is so unspeakable.
Even during the problems in life,
The peace deep within my heart seems unbelievable.

If somehow I could only make you believe,
What a difference knowing Jesus could mean to you.
Then, this good news you'd received,
And within your heart you could have joy, too.

Please don't wait until it is too late.
Trust Christ as your Lord this very day.
Time is drawing nigh, and the hour is at hand.
For Jesus to return from His Heavenly land.

Sandy Anderson

POETIC TREASURES

"Keep on preaching, preacher man.

Stump your feet and raise your hand."

How then shall they call on Him in whom they

have not believed? And how shall they believe in

Him of who they have not heard? And how shall

they hear without a preacher?

Romans 10:14   NKJV

EXPRESSING FAITH AND HOPE

My Thanks to the Preacher

Keep on preaching, preacher man.
How our hearts are filled with glee.
How our souls are challenged to bend a knee.
Keep on preaching, preacher man.
Stump your feet and raise your hand.

If your light goes out, where will we be?
If you quit, who will preach to me?
I need direction, conviction and to be told right.
Keep on preaching, preacher man.
Preach the Word with all your might.

Regardless of what this world has to say.
God's model for the church is the only way.
Keep proclaiming the Word and be strong.
Keep on preaching, preacher man.
Your life is a symbol of right in a world that glorifies wrong.

Sandy Anderson

*This poem is dedicated to my two brothers, Pastor David Anderson, Pastor Robert Anderson, and brother-in-law, Pastor Bernard Fuller.

"Only God can change the quiet voices

That only we can hear.

Foreign to many, to Him revealed;

The essence of our deepest fear."

EXPRESSING FAITH AND HOPE

Whispers

Do you hear the silent whispers in the dark
That we often take to bed?
Isn't our world really our imagination,
And what we perceive in our head?

Hear the silent whispers
When the lights go out?
What are they saying to you?
The answer will reveal what you are about,
And even your point of view.

Only God can change the quiet voices
That only we can hear.
Foreign to many, to Him revealed;
The essence of our deepest fear.

Sandy Anderson

"Now, when I come to the church of God,

As He leads onward, I trod."

I was glad when they said to me,

"Let us go into the house of the Lord."

Psalm 122:1 NKJV

EXPRESSING FAITH AND HOPE

What the Church Means to Me

The church means more than the pulpit furniture,
The pews, the carpet on the floor, and the
Welcome mat at the door.

The church means more to me than the lights in the ceiling,
Candles and beautiful chandeliers.
The church increases my faith
And diminishes my fears.

The church means more than
The flowers around the altar,
The musical instruments,
And all the medley.

Now, when I come to the church of God,
As He leads onward, I trod.
My sisters and brothers, you see,
I am lifted by your testimony.

I love to sing God's praises.
I still my heart, and bow my head, as the prayers are said.
I hear the scripture as read.
I listen to what the preacher said.

The church has given me an opportunity,
To share my talent, time and money.
The church teaches me right from wrong,
And that I am not alone.

Now, lest I forget, the church means communion with the saints.
The bread that represents Jesus' body,
And the blood represented in the wine.
For I must stay connected to the true vine.

Icie Anderson Jackson

"When it is time, we go happily on our way.

Thanking our God, for giving us a new day."

EXPRESSING FAITH AND HOPE

Our Early Walk

As we go for our early walk,
We meet people, give out tracts. and talk.
We talked about various things.
We talked about our world and the people that live therein.
We talked about Jesus Christ, our special friend.

We talked about the flowers that blossom and grass that grow.
We also talked about the snow.
We talked about the old and the young.
We talked about things that use to be and things to come.

We talked about the good and the bad.
We talked about the things that make us happy,
And the things that make us sad.
When it is time, we go happily on our way.
Thanking our God, for giving us a new day.

Icie Anderson Jackson

"A family that prays together stays together.

Thus, it has been said.

But did you know, that in every Christian family,

Christ should be the head."

EXPRESSING FAITH AND HOPE

Christ Should Be The Head

A family that prays together stays together.
Thus, it has been said.
But did you know, that in every Christian family,
Christ should be the head.

Well, you think, what difference would it make,
If Jesus were the head.
For one, in every family,
There would be a happy husband and wife in bed.

Not a mother and lover,
Or a father and friend.
But a husband and wife,
Determined to serve Christ to the end.

Perhaps in every family, if Jesus were the head,
Parents would be an example to the children they bore.
Teaching them to be faithful to church,
Where they could hear the Word and not have to search.

Parents through serving Christ,
Would show their children that Jesus is their only hope.
Not rock and roll, rap or soul,
Or foolish cults, booze or dope.

But isn't it sad that many won't believe,
That Jesus is the way.
And for misleading their children and rejecting His truth,
They will have to answer to Him on Judgment Day.

Sandy Anderson

"He could have called a legion of angels

To deliver Him when things got rough.

He could have choose not to be uncomfortable,

But what would have happened to us?"

For God so love the world that He gave His only

begotten Son that whosoever believes in him,

shall not perish but have everlasting life.

John 3:16   NKJV

EXPRESSING FAITH AND HOPE

What Cost Will You Pay?

What a cost God's only Son did pay
By sacrificing His very all.
Yet, we don't even give Him the honor
By having a daily devotion, however small.

What a price He paid for you and me.
He gave up His glory, His honor, His might.
What a price He paid for us who are unworthy.
He suffered and died without a fight.

He could have called a legion of angels
To deliver Him when things got rough.
He could have choose not to be uncomfortable,
But what would have happened to us?

What will we give to show our gratitude
For the Savior and His love?
What sacrifice will we render,
Or will we simply ignore our Savior above?

What cost will you pay for God's dear Son?
Will you stop at a headache or convenient excuse?
What sacrifice will you make to show Him your love?
Will you give Him your life as a vessel to use?

Sandy Anderson

"We locked arms and held hands,

Hoping the world would understand.

We prayed, and we sang along the way,

"We'll Overcome Someday, Oh Yes!

We'll Overcome Someday."

Chapter 2

THOUGHTFUL MOMENTS

I Was There

In the year 1963, for the first time,
I came to the nation's capital, Washington, D.C.
I involved myself in the Civil Right's March,
But I didn't march alone.
The parade was one hundred thousand strong.

I marched because I believed civil rights.
To be for all people, not just a chosen few.
I marched to demonstrate my view.
It was a hot summer day,
But I marched all the way.

My body was tired and perspiration ran down my brow,
As I sat in the street, to rub my weary feet.
Oh, how much they did swell.
But now, over thirty years later,
I have a story to tell.

We locked arms and held hands,
Hoping the world would understand.
We prayed, and we sang along the way,
"We'll Overcome Someday, Oh Yes! We'll Overcome Someday.

We finally arrived at the Lincoln Memorial,
To witness another thing.
We heard, "I Have A Dream," by Martin Luther King.
He was a friend of mine and a brother in Christ.
I am grateful to have had such a friend in my life.

Icie Anderson Jackson

"We went to the climax of the Anderson and

Jackson event... Then home, we were on our way

rejoicing and thanking the Lord for another

glorious day. February the 2nd 1969, is just

another day we shall keep in mind."

*So here is how the story continued, both families
moved on to other churches, and twenty five years
later, Richard and Icie married and have
spent the last twenty years together. They found
each other after both of their spouses passed away.
God works in mysterious ways!*

THOUGHTFUL MOMENTS

Installation Service

Installation service for the Andersons and Jacksons,
February the 2nd, 1969, I shall remember I must be on time.
The church was as pretty as could be with fresh flowers, a newly
painted wall and a well-polished floor from the pulpit to the door.

The Ushers dressed in white, and there job done just right.
Brother D.J. rushed me in on the one note. I hardly had time to hang
my coat. But I didn't mind for I should have been on time.
How I want to apologize for being late,
Believe me, I'm sorry to have made you wait.

The choir dressed in black to put on their act,
And to them I must tell, you did sang very well.
The minister dressed in his robe, the message was food for our soul.
His subject was, "God Has A Man."
He preached like Paul. We were so elated.
We just praised God for all, and so many nice things were said,
But we refuse to let them go to our head.

The Congregation filled the church sincerely and true. Without you,
Round Oak, our day perhaps would have been lonely and blue. You
are wonderful people to know.
Even though, we may not always tell you so.

When the service was over down to the Recreation Center
We went, to the climax of the Anderson and Jackson event,
And what a treat with good food to eat. Then home, we were on our
way, rejoicing and thanking the Lord for another glorious day.
February the 2nd 1969, is just another day we shall keep in mind.

Icie Anderson Jackson

"Sadam lost the battle he thought he had.

Thanks to our service men and women

Of the red, white and blue.

America, land of beauty,

Our colors came shining through."

THOUGHTFUL MOMENTS

Operation Desert Storm

The war we fought is now over,
And we are glad.
Sadam lost the battle he thought he had.
Thanks to our service men and women
Of the red, white and blue.
America, land of beauty, our colors came shining through.

Hopefully, it won't be long
Before our troops are ready to come home.
Thanks again for fighting until the end.
You made it possible for the big win.

Our hearts feel sorrow, for those that
Were not quite as blessed.
To have their love ones,
Survive with all the rest.

To preserve the Kuwaitis rights,
The American troops were ordered to fight.
Was declared on the ground, air or sea.
America, we are proud of thee.

We thank God for answering prayer.
We thank Him for being here.
We thank Him for being there.

Icie Anderson Jackson

"Did I tell you that I went to the

Nixon Inaugural Ball?

This floor was so slippery I though I would fall.

We were packed in there like sardine fish,

But I didn't mind for we got our wish."

THOUGHTFUL MOMENTS

Nixon's Inaugural Ball

Did I tell you that I went to the Nixon Inaugural Ball?
This floor was so slippery I thought I would fall.
We were packed in there like sardine fish,
But I didn't mind for we got our wish.

I was shocked when my husband invited me to go.
One of my co-workers encouraged me right out the door.
One said it would be nice, but he didn't consider the price.
Another one told me to go home for it was time.
I then left, leaving my co-workers behind.

Anyway, to the Ball I went, and our money we spent.
But it was great to be among the crowd.
Even though, perspiration ran down my brow.
The Washington Hilton was as pretty as a dream.
But things aren't always, as they sometimes seem.

Spiritual music is my favorite you know,
But I must admit I did enjoy the show.
The honor was mine the President to see,
His wife, Pat, and family. Agnew was present to celebrate, too,
And other VIPs stood so near, the opportunity was mine to share.

When everything was over, we left like a flash.
We were happy that we had souvenirs for our sash.
We stopped and had breakfast. Then, home we flew
With our stomachs full, but sleepy and tired too.

January 20, 1969, I shall remember for a very long time.
It was my first time attending an Inaugural Ball.
I guess I never will tell it all. What a wonderful night we spent.
We were privileged to attend this great, historical event.

Icie Anderson Jackson

"There is a warm spirit in my soul.

My mind is still young.

Yet, I am getting old.

But, I am still travelling on preparation road."

THOUGHTFUL MOMENTS

My Birthday

November is my birthday month, and others too,
So here is what I'll do.
I'll celebrate today in a Christian way,
And even throughout the night,
I'll continue in God's light.

November is my birthday month
And maybe yours as well.
So I'll stand and tell
That I feel good
To be a part of the sisterhood.

I've lived through the good times and the bad.
My heart has been happy, and it has been sad.
I've witnessed things I have never witnessed before.
Thus, I shall never witness anymore.

November is my birthday month, even though, it is cold.
There is a warm spirit in my soul.
My mind is still young.
Yet, I am getting old.
But, I am still travelling on preparation road.
Heaven shall be my end,
If I should keep my trust in Him.

Icie Anderson Jackson

"Can you imagine how nice it will be?

When America can claim to be war-free."

THOUGHTFUL MOMENTS

I Wonder

Sometimes I wonder how long it will be,
'til Operation Desert Storm's end become a reality.
Hopefully, it will not be long
'til our troops can pack up and come home.
Can you imagine how nice it will be?
When America can claim to be war-free.
We must admit war is destructive,
How well do we know?
Look around; it's beginning to show.
If war there must be,
America, we are praying for thee.
We shall liberate Kuwait,
Even though many lives it may take.

Icie Anderson Jackson

"Thank you for all your spiritual fervency.

We shall continue your Godly legacy.

We love you, daddy!!"

*My siblings and I wrote this poem for my dad's home going in 1987. He was an awesome Christian father who tried to live an exemplary life. He loved people and his family.

THOUGHTFUL MOMENTS

*Our Tribute To Dad

Dad, you mean the world to us.
We'll think about you everyday,
And in our hearts, you will always know,
That we love you in a special way.

You live within us and always will,
And though you are gone, we love you still.
While it is true that we remain here on earth,
We shall lead others to the second birth.

Our lives are a witness of your faithful prayers,
And we are proud and grateful to be your heirs.
We dedicate our lives to uplifting your Lord
Proclaiming the Word, which is a two-edged sword.

We shall see you in heaven on some glorious day.
Our Lord will call us, too,
Because we are not here to stay.
Thank you for all your spiritual fervency.
We shall continue your Godly legacy.

We love you, daddy!!

The Anderson Children,
Robert, Jr., Sandra, Brenda, David

"My father was like an angel as he lived here on earth

I can hear his voice and see his smile, and

I am so glad I was his child.

My father was like an angel."

THOUGHTFUL MOMENTS

My Father Was Like An Angel

My father was like an angel as he lived here on earth.
He would always sit at the kitchen table and talk to me,
Trying to pour wisdom in my head.
I sat up and paid attention, and now I live what daddy said.

My father was like an angel as he lived here on earth.
He would pray at the alter, and
He would put his hand on my head.
I now realize the meaning, but then, I was only a kid.

My father was like an angel as he lived here on earth.
He never let us out of his reach, and
Always had a lesson to teach.
And every single summer, he would take us to play at the beach.

My father was like an angel as he lived here on earth
I can hear his voice and see his smile, and
I am so glad I was his child.
My father was like an angel.

Sandy Anderson

"Now what they have grown to be,

is our contribution to humanity."

Chapter 3

LOVE, LEAVE AND LIKE

My First Love, Robert

I met my husband Robert in my sister's grocery store,
After which our love began to grow.
Robert went back to school
To learn more about the Christian rule.
We corresponded like most young lovers do,
Hoping and praying one day our dreams would come true.
That day finally came when Robert proposed,
And I accepted as though I had discovered gold.
And off to the preacher we went, and our $5.00 we spent.
Our firstborn, Robert Jr., was a baby boy.
He brought much happiness and joy.
And then came Sandra Maxine;
And Brenda was a dream.
We thought we were finished,
But God said, "No, I want to bless you again,"
That's when David to the world came in.
Now, what they have grown to be is our contribution to humanity.
Thank you, Honey.

Icie Anderson Jackson

"My love for your is genuine,

And it is my desire to express it with zeal.

My desire is to be a reality;

To experience a love totally real."

LOVE, LEAVE AND LIKE

A Love Totally Real

Yes, we fell in love.
Is that a sin?
Maybe it did happen before our minds could comprehend.
What the heck, love is from within.
I refuse to allow myself to regret the path my heart has taken.
I must be honest with myself,
For this is reality, and I am awakened.
So why the apprehension?
Why should I dismay?
Are you churning up my waters?
Moving me as the sunray?

Don't play with my emotions.
What I need is your devotion.
If you don't desire to be in my life,
Why jab at my heart with a knife?

Please, walk out of my life, walk out of my life,
If your love is not real.
My love for your is genuine,
And it is my desire to express it with zeal.
My desire is to be a reality;
To experience a love totally real.

Sandy Anderson

"Tomorrow may not be ours to say.

Our security is only to love more in our day."

LOVE, LEAVE AND LIKE

Together Today

We are together today.
How long will you stay?
My heart grows fonder each and everyday.

I care today.
What do you say?
For we are bonded by our words.

We need each other today.
Will your caress be a delay?
Our bodies need warmth to in the cold stay.

Darling, let us have today.
Tomorrow may not be ours to say.
Our security is only to love more in our day.

Sandy Anderson

POETIC TREASURES

"Search deep within yourself.

Make up your mind.

Know what you want.

Then, either walk in or walk out."

LOVE, LEAVE AND LIKE

Walk In or Walk Out

So, you think I can't do without you.
Oh, don't fool yourself.
My life existed before you came.
Thus, with you, my darling, I can do without.
Leave me, leave me, go ahead walk away.
After you exit, when you look back, see it I dismay.

Sure, my dear, I love you.
But don't thing you control my mind.
For I was in control when you entered, and
I will be in control when you are behind.
Stay with me if you love me.
Infatuation, I can do without.
What I need is sincere love and devotion,
Not a love full of doubt.

Don't stay with me on my account.
Search deep within yourself.
Make up your mind.
Know what you want.
Then, either walk in or walk out.

Sandy Anderson

POETIC TREASURES

"I asked and asked, would someone please,

Help me to see?

Repeatedly, I was given the answer,

This is the way it is suppose to be."

Beware lest anyone cheat you through

philosophy and empty deceit,

according to the tradition of men...

Colossians 2:8 NKJV

Chapter 4

GLOBAL VIEWS IN RHYME

A Little Girl In Africa

There is a little girl in Africa,
Who will be circumcised today.
Her grandmother will carry her from home,
To cut her clitoris away.

The little girl will scream and holler,
And she won't understand
Why the whole village is in celebration
Carrying out the traditions of man.

Why, I asked, did this little girl loose her sexuality?
To understand this long tradition just seems so foreign to me.
I asked and asked, would someone please, help me to see?
Repeatedly, I was given the answer,
This is the way it is suppose to be.

Sandy Anderson

A little boy in a war torn land,

He cried, it is hard to see my purpose in life.

There is destruction everywhere I see.

...will I someday be set free? "

GLOBAL VIEWS IN RHYME

A Little Boy in a War Torn Land

I asked a little boy in a war torn land,
Why are you so sad?
He said, "Because of all this killing,
It has really made me mad.

He said, month after month, a new loved one dies.
Now, we are down to three.
The fighting has killed my mother and father.
Now, it is just my brother, sister and me.

He cried, it is hard to see my purpose in life.
There is destruction everywhere I see.
Is this the only world for which I must dwell?
Or from bloodshed and destruction, will I someday be set free?

Sandy Anderson

"I was born into an Indonesian brothel,

And evil I am told to do.

Lord, how do I escape my lot,

or is it here I should find you?"

Where can I go from your Spirit? Or where can I

flee from Your presence? If I ascend into heaven,

You are there. If I make my bed in hell,

behold, you are there.

Psalms 139:7-8

GLOBAL VIEWS IN RHYME

Lord, How Do I Escape My Lot?

I was born into an Indonesian brothel, and evil I am told to do.
Lord, how do I escape my lot, or is it here I should find you?
I was born into the slums of India, and I search daily in the trash
for food to eat.
Lord, how do I escape my lot, or is it here we will meet?
I was born a girl in China, and my parents denied me because I was
not a boy.
Lord, how do I escape my lot, and where am I supposed to find your
joy?
I was born a girl in South Africa, and the old men want me to take
their AIDS away.
Lord, how do I escape my lot, or do I accept that I will die from AIDS
today?
I was born in an American ghetto, and there I here a gunshot
every day.
Lord, how do I escape my lot, and how do I learn to trust you in a
special way?
I was born a little boy in an orphanage in Haiti and the alternative
is to be on the street.
Lord, how do I escape my lot when every night my caregiver expects
for sex we are to meet?
I was born in a slum in South America, and my father needed money
so he sold me away.
How do I escape my lot when I have to change hands everyday?
How do I escape my lot when I did not ask to be born this day?
How do I escape my lot when I did not ask to be born in this way?
How do I escape my lot when the entire land around me is poor?
How do I escape my lot without an open door?
How do I escape my lot when the land is filled with violence?
How do escape my lot when the wailing cannot be silenced?

Sandy Anderson

POETIC TREASURES

"Doing what every good mother does

In caring for her young.

She toils endlessly to accomplish her task

Because to survive is to be strong."

She seeks wool and flax, and willingly works with

her hands. She is like the merchant ships, she

brings food from afar. She also rises while it is yet

night, and provides food for her household...

Proverbs 31:13-15   NKJV

GLOBAL VIEWS IN RHYME

African Flip Flops

Flip flops and colorful garments
Is what you are likely to see.
As you watch the African women
Strolling through the village
Natural, hard-working and very pretty.

The ladies work with such complexity
With their babies tied on their backs.
Their manner of grace awes me
As they stroll with ten pound baskets
Balanced on their heads like hats.

Amazingly moving down the street
As if walking in step without a stop
Head held high balancing water pots
Without spilling a single drop.

Doing what every good mother does
In caring for her young.
She toils endlessly to accomplish her task
Because to survive is to be strong.
She adapts to whatever conditions prevail.
However, she may have been done wrong.

Flip flops roaming dusty streets,
Little food to eat,
Families needing to be fed,
Numbers exceeding available beds,
Everywhere needing more supplies,
More flip flops, flip flops, flip flops.

Sandy Anderson

Chapter 5

SOMETHING TO PONDER

The Man of the House

So your daddy left when you were young.
Your mother by several men was done wrong.
You had to drop out of school to work,
Only to be called by family and friends, a stupid jerk.

At the age of nine, you just couldn't cope.
So your uncle turned you on to dope.
While on the corner, you discovered even your preacher smoked.
Now you feel, there is definitely no hope.

You want your little sister to have a chance.
You become strict, and don't allow her to dance.
Instead you want her to enjoy fine clothes and books,
And to supply her with such,
You take up with the crooks.

In time, you want to change, but you get hooked.
You tell yourself, there is a better way.
You tell yourself, in the ghetto, you can't stay,
And that you have to get away.

But you worry about your little brother, sister and mother.
So in your mind, you decided to stay,
And plan to leave with them one day.
So you continue to hang with the crooks
To supply your sister and brother with books.

SOMETHING TO PONDER

The Man of the House (2)

Your momma while drunk tries to kill herself with a knife.
After this, you become determined to shelter
Your little sister and brother from the harshness of ghetto life.
Your momma is grateful for the clothes and books
She thinks you bought.

But pain filled her grateful eyes, when the next day,
you got caught.
She held your sister and brother closely
As the police carried you on the day
While you tried to explain to the cops that it was the only way.

So now in jail you have to watch the mice,
To pay for your sinful vice.
Still in the ghetto, your sister got bit by a mouse.
But you are helpless,
And now your little brother at nine is the man of the house.

Sandy Anderson

"Momma, there's a problem in our community

That nobody wants to talk about.

The men folks mess with the boys and girls

Stroking on thighs and their hidden curls."

SOMETHING TO PONDER

Momma, Why?

Momma, there's a problem in our community
That nobody wants to talk about.
The men folks mess with the boys and girls
Stroking on thighs and their hidden curls.

Some children say they can't even sleep at night
Because as soon as the lights go out,
They have to rear up and fight.

The children say it might be anyone
Looking for a little fun
But usually a cousin, uncle or theirs Momma's boyfriend
Are the regulars who try to come in.

Momma, people just turning their heads
And making excuses.
Even in their own family,
They see all kinds of abuses.

Momma, why doesn't anybody do anything
To help these children in all their pain?
Is it because you were once like these children
And don't feel there is much to gain?

Momma, why?

Sandy Anderson

"America is a melting pot indeed.

We are a people from all persuasions.

We must collaborate to succeed."

SOMETHING TO PONDER

America, So Sweet

America, America, your stolen waters are so sweet.
Regret to the Native American
On whose land I place my feet.

I acquired it by birthright.
My descendants were brought.
Now, I claim it as home.
For my liberty, many have fought.

It's my home to stay.
For my heritage was taken away.
I am sorry, dear Native.
I love this land today.

We must learn from your secrets
In caring for the land.
Lest it be destroyed on every side
Because freedom says we can.

Know this land is ours.
America is a melting pot indeed.
We are a people from all persuasions.
We must collaborate to succeed.

Sandy Anderson

Some will tell you that they made themselves

what they are today.

They would tell you that those sorry people,

Just happen to be born that way.

Every good gift and every perfect gift is from

above, and comes down from the Father of

lights...

James 1:17   NKJV

SOMETHING TO PONDER

Thank God, It Isn't Me

Some will tell you that they made themselves
What they are today.
They would tell you that those sorry people,
Just happen to be born that way.
The babies crying, children dying,
Mothers wailing sorrows untold.
But that is their problem.
I got me and mine.
I got bills to pay;
A place to stay;
A family to love;
And food to eat;
A car to clean;
A play to see;
Clothes to wear;
And an appointment for my hair.
I live in my world,
And that is their life.
I can't say it no plainer,
Or the writing on the wall, you will see;
Thank God, Thank God,
Thank God, that isn't me.

Sandy Anderson

"Feel no shame, Sisters of Sheba, God gave you

your beautiful browns, your black flowered

bosom, your voluptuous African buttocks, your

bold thighs, and your charitable heart."

I am dark, but lovely. O daughters of Jerusalem,

like the tents of Kedar,

like the curtains of Solomon.

Song of Solomon 1:5

SOMETHING TO PONDER

The Beauty of the Black Woman

So defined are the contours of her anatomy,
And the power of her soul.
As she moves, she strolls.
As she sings, she rolls.

Feel no shame, descendants of Sheba.
For you are descendants of a legacy.
A legacy, which began as Sister Eve bore the world's first child,
Which occurred from a love affair, which was surely totally wild.

Arise, queens of comeliness, hold your head up high.
As the world tries to mock and hide your beauty.
For you are everything women hope to be.
And from the world's stereotypes,
you have to break free.

You have been called promiscuous only because men could never
overcome the beauty of your spirit,
And the sensuality you process done so mysteriously.
Feel no shame, Sisters of Sheba. God gave you your beautiful
browns, your black flowered bosom, your voluptuous African
buttocks, your bold thighs, and your charitable heart.
All people, though they may deny it, are cognizant of your beauty.

Arise and walk as an African queen.
For you are the symbol of all beauty,
And what makes you so very special,
Is you do it so naturally!

Sandy Anderson

"It all happen to my momma, you see,

So I guess this is the way it is supposed to be."

SOMETHING TO PONDER

I Guess This Is the Way It's Suppose To Be

Please ignore the pains and bruises.
Please ignore the kicks and tears.
Please ignore my busted eye and lip.
Please don't mind my running blood.

I got a small baby and three other children.
Who need clothes, shelter and food.
I can live with the pitiful stares,
As long as my man returns here upstairs.

You see, he works at times and gets angry,
And then, other times he drinks.
It all happen to my momma, you see,
So I guess this is the way it is suppose to be.

Sandy Anderson

"Poetry allows me to cry without tears, and speak without discussion. It allows me to feel in words."

ABOUT THE AUTHORS

Sandra Anderson has been an educator for over twenty years. She grew up listening to her mother's poetry and wrote this book as a tribute to her. Sandra has written poetry and has published various articles throughout the years, but her career life has been spent in working education and volunteer work in international service.

In 1984, Sandra spent a summer in Sudan, Africa as a team member with Operation Crossroads Africa. This trip was to get Africa out of her system. She said, "The soil of Africa was calling her." This trip would change her life forever. As she recalls, "When I landed in Sudan and travel to our living quarters, I remember I looked around and thought I was on another planet. It was so different from everything I ever knew."

Sandra served as a pastor's wife for twenty-five years and has a son and daughter. In the midst of her busy life as an educator, she co-founded two churches, founded a pre-school, started and developed the curriculum for a high school International Studies Program and founded Educators International Service, Inc. to led educators and students in serving internationally and connecting educationally with schools around the world.

Sandra has led teams to different countries. In the summer of 1994, while working with Operation Crossroads Africa as a team leader, Sandra went to The Gambia, West Africa. After being there for about a month, the country underwent a coup. A young military general ousted out the prime minister and came to power. After going through several checkpoints at gunpoint and experiencing the change of a government, Sandra led her team safely out of it because she knew that the God she served would get her home to her family.

Spending a lot of time traveling and living in Africa and spending so many years serving in ministry, a lot of Sandra's poems deal with these experiences. When asked about why she wrote poetry about such serious topics, she said, "Poetry allows me to cry without tears, and speak without discussion. It allows me to feel in words."

POETIC TREASURES

"Her children rise up and call her blessed..."

Psalms 31:28

ABOUT THE AUTHORS

Icie Anderson Jackson was born in Hinze, Mississippi. She moved to Harrisburg, Pennsylvania before her teen years in order to finish her education in high school. Opportunities to go pass the eighth grade were very limited to African Americans in Hinze, Mississippi. There in Pennsylvania, she not only finished high school, but found her first love, the late Rev. Robert J. Anderson, Sr.

Due to Robert's transfer, in 1965, they moved to Maryland with their three children. Shortly after, as a pastor's wife, Icie began to perform skits and recitations at churches and in different events throughout the country. One of her poems is featured in the *World Treasury of Great Poems*, 1989 Edition. Throughout the years, she has received recognition and awards for her recitations and skits.

Icie was born right after the Great Depression and lived through the Civil Rights era. In 1963, she participated in the March on Washington with the late Rev. Robert Anderson, Sr. who was a friend to Dr. Martin Luther King, Jr. This is the story behind the poem, I Was There, as she talks about the impact that the March on Washington had on her life.

After being married to Robert Anderson for thirty three years, she laid her first love to rest, but only to be comforted five years later when on June 18, 1994, she married a dear friend, Richard Jackson, after his wife died.

Icie worked and served faithfully as a pastor's wife as she raised four children, two girls, Sandra and Brenda, and two boys, David and Robert. Along with her husband, Richard, who has six children. They have ten children, almost thirty grandchildren and ten great grandchildren.

Later in 1990, she made a video for the water company she worked with for twenty four years called, The Genesis of Tobacco. It encouraged many people to quit smoking. From a little girl from Hinze, Mississippi to Washington, DC, Icie has shaken five president's hands. She has made her impact through her charm and poetry and through her children who have traveled the world in building bridges, missions, reconciliations and humanitarian work.

Made in the USA
Charleston, SC
07 May 2014